TABLE OF CONTENTS

WHAT IS PERSONAL BRANDING?

We all are familiar with the desire to be perceived in a certain way. Essentially, personal branding is nothing more of the same but applied in a broader context. For a professional, a personal brand defines their unique selling point to employers and clients and is used to promote themselves.

If you want to build a personal brand, you should be able to distinguish yourself from the competition with your personality, experience, and unique skills. It not only reflects your story as a person but also represents how you conduct yourself in spoken and unspoken words, i.e., your behaviour and attitude.

When you are able to perfect the art of branding, you can tie your persona with the job role and position you are seeking. You can make the world believe as if you were born for the very role, demanding everybody to recognize you the way you see yourself.

However, being overzealous in your approach can be more harmful than helpful. You must maintain a subtle and balanced line of action to brand yourself successfully. To perfect the art of personal branding, first, you must understand what people may regard as your personal brand.

In the corporate world, your personal brand represents your image. This image can be a combination of how people look at you in real life and the impression they get by reading information about you online.

You can design your personal brand like an architect and then build it brick by brick to suit your desired role. How can you develop a great personal brand? Remember the time the internet was not mainstream? Back then, corporate professionals used business cards to promote their personal brands.

However, after the advent of the internet, especially social media, things have changed drastically now. The world has now become far more connected and globalized. Thus, social media platforms provide you with the opportunity to build and promote your personal brand and gain an edge over your competition.

WHY IS PERSONAL BRANDING IMPORTANT IN THE AGE OF SOCIAL MEDIA?

Social media has now become an essential part of our lives. Whether you use it for personal or business use, the fact is that we are living in the age of social media. In fact, As of July 2019, the total number of active social media users was 3.534 billion.

If you're familiar with how social media sites work, you would know that people generally comment, share, and follow the posts of users they find intriguing. Similarly, it is the best platform for individuals to express and share their ideas, views and information with their personal and professional contacts. So, if you want the world to know about you, social media is the best place to kickstart your personal brand career and attract prospective employers.

Most employers start screening potential candidates from the moment they appear on their radar. They conduct thorough online research on prospective employees to find the best fit for their organizations. Some surveys even suggest that about 70 per cent of employers use social media as a measure to screen candidates during the hiring process.

Most people consider social media as a platform where anything goes or can be shared as long as it is relevant to their personal views. However, keep in mind that your current or prospective employer or client might be keeping an eye on your social media accounts. You should refrain from venting about your problems on your social media accounts. If you are into sharing your opinions on social media, try to keep the conversation light and politically neutral.

Instead, you can use your social media profile as a launching pad for your personal brand. You can use it to demonstrate your knowledge, qualifications, experience and skills in your respective field. In many ways, it is one of the few places where you can make yourself distinguishable without meeting anyone.

You can witness the practical effectiveness of this approach with the rise of influencer marketing in recent years. For instance, the infographic from The Shelf indicates that 92% of consumers prefer recommendations from unknown influencers online over brand content. This has led to a huge shift in how businesses market themselves and their products and services. As a result, companies are using social media to personalize their businesses and differentiate themselves from others. While this has been easier for small businesses, even large organizations have tried their hand at leveraging social media for marketing.

When it comes to individuals who made the most of personal branding, Steve Jobs is the first name that comes to mind. Jobs distinguished himself as the face of Apple even before the phrase itself became relevant. Nowadays, we see more of Elon Musk's personal brand on the news than Tesla's corporate brand.

Similarly, you will see owners of many other multi-million brands bonding with potential customers on social media before they deliver the company's message. Therefore, it's only smart for aspiring professionals to make the most of social media for developing their personal brands.

COMMON CHALLENGES IN PERSONAL BRANDING

While social media provides you with the best opportunity to make a mark for yourself in the corporate world, presenting yourself as an accomplished individual is not an easy task. There are limited job openings and countless professionals competing for them. So, it is no surprise that you may face several challenges to build a unique and strong personal brand.

Creating a personal brand requires deep introspection and self-reflection. Unless you don't understand your needs, goals, personality, strengths and weaknesses, it will be extremely difficult for you to market yourself successfully. Although most people know themselves well, others are left searching for the right words to describe themselves.

If you want to work on your personal brand in order to get a certain job position, you must learn about the requirements of that role. Afterwards, you must work on the attributes that your target audience expects and build your personal brand around that position.

This can be a major challenge for most people who like staying in their own circle. Generally, introverts often find it hard to express themselves in the way that personal branding demands. Thus, they are unable to make full use of their expertise and build a strong identity for themselves.

However, this isn't always the case. On many occasions, extroverts can become overzealous in their efforts to create personal brands. They try too hard, lose their subtleness, and come across as 'salesy.'

Although selectively showcasing your positive side can offer you the best chance of getting the attention of employers, companies, or clients, taking it too far can surely backfire. No one wants to hire someone who pretends to be something they are not.

Employers, nowadays, are well aware of the people who are self-proclaimed experts but fail to get the job done after they are hired. Therefore, it's important to distance yourself from the image of such professionals and appear as original and authentic as you can.

The key to success is in remaining authentic to your true self and highlighting your strengths. You need to present yourself as an individual who understands the requirements and complexities of the desired position and has the knowledge and skills to succeed in the given role.

Last but not least, it is important to understand that building and maintaining an effective personal brand requires a lot of effort, time and patience. Your goal should be on making a lasting impression on your target audience – prospective employer, clients, etc. – by offering real value to them.

BRANDING ON LINKEDIN

W hen people talk about social media, they tend to focus on Instagram, Facebook, Twitter, and YouTube. However, for an aspiring professional who wants to build a personal brand, LinkedIn is the ultimate social networking platform.

As more and more people are leveraging the internet to market their professional skills, they realize that LinkedIn is the perfect social platform to connect with people who have similar professional interests.

Not long ago, LinkedIn was considered to be a platform where people uploaded their resumes and sought a chance to interact with employers. However, over the years, LinkedIn has proved to be a social network for both influencer marketing and online advertisement.

While this may seem like an opportunity only for businesses, its benefits trickle down to the individual level. Those who are seeking to gain recognition can use LinkedIn to connect with other companies, businesses, world-famous influencers, and leading authors. It is like a one-stop-shop for fresh graduates, experienced professionals and entrepreneurs to market themselves, reach out to others and build long-lasting relationships with them.

Read on to understand why you should choose LinkedIn for advocating your personal brand:

LinkedIn Market Solutions

After the purchase of Microsoft in 2016, LinkedIn has increased its advertising offerings gradually. Marketers can now try several options, such as Text Ads, Dynamic Ads, Programmable Display Ads, Sponsored InMail, and Sponsored Content, to expand their marketing efforts.

They also have the option to review the performance of their marketing efforts by making the most of features like Conversion Tracking, Lead Generation, Website Demographics, and much more.

Furthermore, useful tools like LinkedIn Insight Tag can help marketers track visitors directed to their pages through their campaigns. This makes it a significantly helpful metric for gauging the results from one's influencer campaigns.

The Foothold for Prominent Influencers

One of the most notable things about LinkedIn is that you can connect to some of the greatest influencers in your domain easily. These influencers possess their own LinkedIn accounts. Although they don't present themselves as influencers on LinkedIn, their success and fame in their respective domains make them the centre of attention on LinkedIn.

One prominent example of this is the Director of Data Science and ML at Gartner, Andriy Burkov. He was the author of the widely popular *The Hundred Page Machine Learning Book* and was included in LinkedIn's Top Voices in 2018. Presently, the author has more than 100,000 followers on LinkedIn, and he continues to keep people informed about the latest developments in data science, analytics, and machine learning.

Even if you do not have a penchant for data science, you can certainly find an influencer you can learn from, who is also relevant to your domain. One of the most exciting things about LinkedIn is that professionals from all corners of the world come here to connect and share ideas and insights with other people. Therefore, you will find all the leading bloggers and domain experts having LinkedIn accounts.

LinkedIn Brand Influencers

Besides well-known authors, bloggers, and domain experts, LinkedIn has also opened its doors to a wide variety of full-time influencers who also represent brands. The social network provides a firm foundation for influencer marketing by allowing these people to operate and endorse their brand through their accounts.

However, becoming an official LinkedIn influencer is not easy. The network follows a thorough research process and stringent selection criteria to shortlist individuals as influencers. According to LinkedIn helpdesk, LinkedIn Influencers are selected via invitation only. The company selects 500+ of the world's leading leaders, thinkers, and innovators.

People recognize these people as leaders in their respective industries and geographies. Being a part of LinkedIn influencers, these people discuss trending topics, such as workplace culture, the prospect of improving higher education, and the wrong steps taken by policymakers.

Understandably, not everyone has the accolades or expertise to touch shoulders with legends like Bill Gates from Microsoft and Richard Branson from Virgin. However, like Andriy Burkov, you can manage to become an expert on any topic if you have the required knowledge and expertise in it.

LINKEDIN FOR PERSONAL BRANDING

A lthough many companies use LinkedIn for corporate branding, it is still the ultimate social network for business professionals. The platform allows individuals to promote their unique skills and strengths to their target audiences. Ultimately, it helps them to build new and retain connections, and move towards greater success in their respective fields.

According to one survey, 80% of LinkedIn users agree that professional networking is one of the most important factors for career growth. Companies realize that LinkedIn's talent pool of 645 million users is the perfect place to find suitable job candidates. The platform even claims that 75% of recruiters said that they were more successful after using LinkedIn for recruitment.

All these figures indicate that the use of a professional networking platform like LinkedIn will only increase further with time. However, to develop a personal brand via LinkedIn, you must know the basic rules to get started. Not only do you need to create a stellar profile and find the right connections on LinkedIn, but also use the resources on the platform to stand out from your competition.

Creating a LinkedIn Profile

To start with, you cannot make use of the opportunities available on LinkedIn unless you create a professional and marketable profile. Creating a strong

LinkedIn profile will set a firm foundation for your personal brand. Later, you can use the power of this platform to contact people you want to reach out to and send them any message you want. The fact that 70% of the total LinkedIn users are based outside the US proves that the platform has gained global acceptance.

What's more interesting is that people who have relatively higher-paying jobs tend to be drawn to LinkedIn. According to a study of the PEW Research Center, 45% of individuals using LinkedIn make over $75,000 annually. Therefore, before seeking a personal brand for yourself , you must first create a profile on LinkedIn. Here are the main steps for creating a LinkedIn profile:

CHOOSE THE RIGHT TYPE
OF ACCOUNT

F irst off, you must be clear about your goals for making a LinkedIn account. If you know what you need to achieve from your account, it will be easier to choose an account type. For instance, if you are looking to promote your business on LinkedIn and want to utilize its features, a Premium Business will help expand your business insights.

On the other hand, an account type, such as Sales Navigator, focuses on business development. It provides companies with the capability to generate leads and save a database for all prospects. Recruiter Lite is for companies that are keen on hiring individuals that fit their requirements.

Lastly, the Premium Career account is tailored to the needs of job seekers. If you are looking to establish a personal brand as a professional, this is the account type you should choose. You can still consider using the Basic account type, which is essentially a toned-down version of the Premium account.

As far as personal branding is concerned, the best accounts to use are Basic and Premium Career. Let's see them in detail:

Basic Account

The Basic account on LinkedIn is free. It allows beginners to use all the basic features they need to start their journey on LinkedIn. You can use the account to build a great profile, find mutual connections, and connect with other people by sending them requests. You also have the option to post different content, such as blogs, articles, and SlideShares.

Premium Career

Premium Career is an upgrade from the Basic plan. Of course, you have the option to utilize social networking services with the Basic account, but if you upgrade to a Career plan, you can get plenty of additional features.

For instance, the account lets you use 'cold calling' on LinkedIn. What this means is that you can directly send a message (InMail) to anyone without having to introduce yourself to them through one of your contacts. As a potential job seeker, this can help you to connect with people you are not formally introduced to and expand your network.

Usually, when you search for someone or perform an advanced search on LinkedIn, the search results are restricted to 10 on a free account. After paying for the first level of the premium account, you can access almost 300 search results and find the companies you were looking for.

Keep in mind; the free account limits the visibility of your profile. It also shows the names of the people or companies who viewed your profile five days ago. The paid account extends that limit to 90 days

Moreover, by choosing the LinkedIn Career premium account, you will gain access to features such as LinkedIn Learning and LinkedIn Salary. Both of these features are extremely useful.

For instance, LinkedIn Salary allows job seekers to track and analyze trends in salaries for different jobs and titles. They can compare their earnings with other potential applicants' salaries. This feature also gives them an idea of the most in-demand skills that they can learn to build a successful career for themselves. If this feature can motivate a professional for further self-improvement, the platform supplements their hunger for growth with the best learning platform: LinkedIn Learning. Linkedin Learning gives you access to countless learning resources. Regardless of which field you belong to, you will find a variety of resources that can help you strengthen your profile.

Furthermore, with these features, professionals can also gain access to unique, valuable, and timely data on specific trends, businesses, and geographic locations.

GETTING THE BASICS COVERED

T he next step is to make sure that the email address you enter for making your profile is the one you regularly use. You also need to be aware of all the connection requests you get to build a strong network. Besides that, it's important not to forget adding key details, such as your basic demographic information.

After that, you can add your phone number so that the people in your network can contact you. If you are a professional looking for better opportunities, adding your number or email to your profile will give potential employers an easier way to contact you. You can edit the contact information anytime.

When you are creating your profile, you can permit LinkedIn to add contacts from your email contact list to your profile. If you don't do this, it will be a bit harder for you to gain traction since you won't have any connections in the beginning.

However, once you have created the profile, LinkedIn will keep prompting you for more information. For instance, the platform will ask for your current employment status. If you are currently unemployed, you might consider using phrases like "currently looking for employment opportunities" to define your purpose for being on LinkedIn.

USE A PROFESSIONAL PHOTO

A s you are creating a LinkedIn profile for a professional audience, the picture you use for your profile should be a professional headshot. If you don't have a professional headshot, make sure that you get one as soon as possible. Use the cleanest, most professional-looking picture of yourself.

Your LinkedIn profile photo will make an impression on potential employers and contacts, so make sure that you pose and dress appropriately for it.

DON'T MISS OUT THE SUMMARY FIELD

The summary field on your profile conveys your journey as a professional. Therefore, it should be true to your experience and relevant to the impression you want to make.

To make the summary more readable, use bullet points. You can think about what your target reader wants to know about you that might attract him or her to your profile. Alternatively, you can also add media files, such as a video, to summarize your professional experience.

ADD DOCUMENTS RELATED TO YOUR EXPERIENCE

Even if you don't want to add an introduction video as a visual representation of your professional career, you can add other media files to represent various facets of your professional life. For instance, if you are a graphic designer, you can add the best pieces from your collection to represent your work. This will make it easier for you to create a visual portfolio, which can go a long way when used along with your standard information.

KEEP WORK HISTORY TO THE POINT

While writing your work experience, it's not necessary to list down every work experience. Since you are designing your LinkedIn profile to keep a certain persona, it's necessary that you keep your main objective in mind.

There's no harm in writing down every work experience you have had during your career, as long as it serves the purpose of facilitating your long-term goals. However, if adding that work experience doesn't add value to the role you are currently pursuing, then it's better to leave that off.

ADD LINKS TO RELEVANT SITES

L inkedIn allows its users to add external links to their profiles. Therefore, you have the opportunity to share your information from other platforms to LinkedIn. However, you have to be careful about what you share. If you intend to share blogs you like or a meme you are fond of, LinkedIn is not the place for it.

Nevertheless, if you write a work-related blog or maintain an online portfolio, then you can utilize the URL links on your profile. For people working as writers, this can be an opportunity to link to the content they have written. Similarly, software developers and programmers can add links to their GitHub page, where they maintain an online portfolio.

However, you can post only three links on your profile. So, you must ensure that these links define your qualifications for your desired role. Alternatively, you can link it to your own personal website or business to help people get more information about you. You can even add links to other social media accounts as long as your posts are insightful and represent a polished mind.

CREATE A CRISP HEADLINE

LinkedIn gives you the option to add a headline. Usually, LinkedIn shows your headline along with your name, current company, or job title. So, it's right up there for anyone to see. Like everything else on your LinkedIn profile, your headline should be relevant to your goals. It should define you and represent what makes your personal brand unique.

When you are writing your headline, consider listing your specialty. You can also experiment by speaking directly with your audience or summarize your expertise in a catchy phrase.

Besides that, if you want to make your headline searchable, it's important to include keywords. You can also use industry jargon, unless it's too complicated for people to understand. Lastly, it's important to limit your headline to 10 words because anything longer than that is not suitable for a headline.

COMPLETE YOUR PROFILE

In the end, you should complete your profile by adding other necessary details to it. These details include information such as your skills, education, and volunteer associations, etc. You can choose to include interesting stuff about yourself that doesn't make it to your resume, but show that you are a well-rounded individual.

However, you should remember that if your volunteer experience directly relates to the role you are seeking, you can include it in your work history. This will help you to show experience in the relevant section, instead of the bottom of your profile.

Showcasing Your Skills Successfully

For better or for worse, now everyone can announce his or her presence on a global platform. LinkedIn, along with other networks, gives people the opportunity to present themselves in the brightest light possible.

People tend to list prominent aspects of their expertise as skills to show their worth for a given role. On a platform like LinkedIn, doing this can help them remain in the top rankings.

In most cases, LinkedIn uses various algorithms to search through your profile and detect various keywords related to what you do. As a result, the skills someone mentions on his or her profile also acts as a keyword for them.

Consequently, these skills can become the means to receive more profile views. As the number of profile views increases, it will be easier for you to gain recognition from others. Companies searching for the skills you possess will likely see your profile whenever they search for them on LinkedIn. Therefore, they are more likely to contact you if you are close to what they expect from a desired candidate.

LinkedIn even claims that if members add five or more skills in their profile, recruiters target are x33 times more likely to contact them. Furthermore, their profile reviews ca increase up to x17 times.

In total, you need to add at least three skills to complete your profile and become a LinkedIn "All-Star." However, you have the option to add as many as 50 skills on your profile. The first ten in these skills are shown with thumbnail images of endorsers (we'll talk about this later) along with them.

Like work experience, it's best to only add skills, depending on the opportunities you are pursuing as a professional. You can add other skills, too; however, you must make sure that only the most relevant ones stay at the top.

LinkedIn maintains a Skills Directory, where it saves the skills it knows about or the ones that people search for most often. You should avoid adding skills like being able to ride a bike without using your hands or anything like that.

You can still add specific skills linked to your domain, business, or industry. However, you have to bear in mind that most people don't search for those skills on LinkedIn. It's essential to keep your stronger suit at the top and ensure that it reflects your image.

LinkedIn even gives you the option to remove certain skills from your list. You can use this option to keep only the skills tailored for the role you desire. All you have to do is click the edit (✎) icon beside the "Add a new skill" option on your profile. After that, click on the trash bin (🗑) next to the skill you want to remove.

Furthermore, you can also change the order of how your skills are displayed on your profile. This can help you realign your most prominent skills at the top. If that wasn't enough, you could also pin three skills as the "Top Skills" on your profile.

LinkedIn aims to create a platform where everyone has access to employment opportunities based on the skills they have. As a result, people are able to benefit from the platform, regardless of their background and degree.

Besides that, the platform enables hiring managers to select candidates tailored for their roles as well. A research by LinkedIn revealed 83% of hiring managers agreed that credentials and skills were getting more and more important for hiring talent. Having said that, 77% of hiring managers also said that it was hard to know which skills the candidates actually possessed without using a skill assessment.

Unfortunately, with so many people using the network, it's extremely difficult for both professionals and hiring managers to find what they need. A study conducted by LinkedIn even showed that 76% of professionals wanted to verify their skills to a potential employer and stand out amongst other candidates. Thanks to LinkedIn, this is no longer a problem for people using the platform.

LinkedIn has introduced a Skill Assessment feature for professionals. Skill Assessment allows professionals on its platform to take standardized, short assessments. This allows these people to validate the skills they showcase on their profile.

Although the Skills Assessment feature is still in the testing phase and not available to every member, it is an effective way for demonstrating your knowledge. Members have to complete a 15-20 multiple choice question assessment to validate their skills on the platform. The platform times each question, and you have to complete them in the given session.

At this stage, the assessment is limited to domains, such as general, tech, and other skills. You have the option to validate any skill you want, from Microsoft Excel to Javascript and Python programming. Several leading industry experts design these assessments to evaluate a person's expertise in a certain area. Other times, subject matter experts source these assessments from LinkedIn Learning's network.

After clearing the skill assessment, the person gets a badge that advocates their level of expertise. Members that score more than the 70th percentile or more can decide whether or not they would like to display the badge on their profile.

The platform gives you the option to attest your knowledge in technical skills like the following topics:

- Java
- HTML
- R
- XML
- Amazon Web Services
- Bash, Hadoop
- Python
- WordPress
- Angular
- Node.js
- Scala
- React.js
- MySQL
- C#
- Git
- JavaScript
- jQuery
- MongoDB
- PHP

And many more.

You can also prove your skills in designing tools and platforms, along with architecture and accounting tools:

- QuickBooks
- Dreamweaver
- Keynote
- Lightroom
- Autodesk Maya
- Revit
- AutoCAD
- ArcGIS
- InDesign
- Final Cut Pro
- Adobe Premiere Pro
- After Effects
- Adobe Illustrator
- Adobe Photoshop
- iMovie
- Avid Media Composer
- SketchUp

In the future, LinkedIn aims to include more skills that can be demonstrated with these kinds of assessments. For instance, the platform may include skills, such as expertise in popular business tools. Hiring managers and recruiters can utilize the skill assessment tool to select suitable candidates more effectively, based on their skills.

HOW CAN SKILL ASSESSMENT HELP YOU?

Since many people tend to overstate the accuracy of their skills on platforms like LinkedIn, it can be difficult to get the attention you need on this platform. Therefore, it's important that you make the most of the options available, such as the Skill Assessment.

A verified badge on your profile can go a long way in distinguishing you from other candidates. Even if you don't pass the multi-choice question test, you have complete control over the results that show up on your profile. As a result, this gives you the opportunity to brush up on your skills and be more prepared.

HOW CAN YOU SHARPEN YOUR SKILLS ON LINKEDIN?

LinkedIn not only allows you to attest to the skills you have gained over the years, but also helps develop new ones. Regardless of whether you pass the assessment or not, the platform will outline how you performed on the test.

In order to help you improve, the platform will give you free access to the LinkedIn Learning course that is relevant to the Skill Assessment test. Although this free access is for a limited time, it can help you to improve the skills displayed on your profile. After you clear the LinkedIn Skill Assessment for an in-demand skill, the platform will let you know if a relevant job recommendation comes by.

Selecting and Prioritizing Your Personal Brand Attributes

The key to building your personal brand is to know your core personal brand attributes. Being aware of these traits can help you to make smarter decisions and focus all your efforts on things that matter most. Moreover, if you know which of your personal brand attributes are the strongest, it would be easier to find the right audience and deliver the message you want to convey.

IDENTIFY YOUR PERSONAL BRAND ATTRIBUTES

A t the basic level, every product has different attributes, which make it unique from other products. These attributes are objective, and indisputable characteristics represent a product's identity.

Similarly, your personal brand may include different attributes, which make you stand among the crowd. However, to promote your personal brand successfully, you have to decide which core attributes need to be highlighted the most.

For that, you must have a clear understanding of who you are. You need to ask yourself which key attributes define you as an individual. Is it your gender, age, nationality, socio-economic background or something else?

After that, you need to look at your professional attributes and identity which role suits you the best. Can you grow as a brand strategist, a software engineer, a writer, or a social media influencer?

Once you are clear about the role that matches your goals and values, you can start thinking about other professional titles or roles that will help you reach your ultimate goal. Nevertheless, once you get the gist of your core attributes, you will have a solid foundation to base your brand identity on.

HOW DO YOUR SKILLS ALIGN WITH YOUR PERSONAL BRAND?

I dentifying your core attributes is necessary. However, no one will consider you until you can prove that you can add value to him or her in some manner. Just like any product, you have to present your technical qualities and functional benefits in order to develop a strong personal brand.

The easiest way to do that is to evaluate the skills you have gained over the years. Your skills and professional qualification represent the value you can bring to an organization. These skills can be anything from technical skills stemmed from knowledge and experience to soft skills that are an inherent part of your personality. Furthermore, you need to see if those skills are relevant to your personal brand.

For that, you need to determine what your three strongest technical or functional skills are. For instance, you can select expertise in certain software technology, project management, and business intelligence as your top three technical skills when searching for a leading role in the software industry. However, you should be genuine in your approach and only consider the roles you have expertise in.

After you have dealt with technical skills, you need to highlight the soft skills that define you the best. This can be anything from your unrelenting work ethic, your ability to work in cross-functional teams, or your persuasive nature. Possessing the right soft skills makes it easier for you to display your technical expertise and grow as a professional.

Regardless of how many skills you have, you have to make sure that you focus on branding the skills that align with your personal brand.

DOES YOUR PERSONALITY MATCH YOUR BRAND?

Besides your core attributes and functional benefits, you can differentiate yourself further by possessing a unique personality or tone of voice. Your personality is the sum of your values, attitude, and behavior.

However, many companies have adopted values and approaches that enable them to connect with a certain mindset and convey emotional experience through their products. For instance, Nike represents the concept of delivering confidence that comes by wearing high-performance apparel.

Similarly, you can emit a charisma that inspires the people around you. However, in your case, the medium for that emotional experience would not be a product. Rather, it would be driven by your personality, philosophies, and principles. Ultimately, your professional behavior and attitude will leave a lasting impression on others.

Nevertheless, you need to be clear about how you want to be known. Do you want to be seen as decisive, friendly, or collaborative? First, you must identify which of these behaviors align with your attributes. After that, you can work on those approaches to make them a strong suit of your personality.

Next, you must set guiding principles that serve as a compass throughout your career. These principles may drive your career decisions, the products you want to endorse, or the type of organization you want to associate yourself with. Furthermore, it can also affect how you conduct work or live your life.

Acting in a way that's inconsistent with your values can tarnish your reputation and damage others' perception of you. Therefore, you must be careful about which values you choose to highlight in your personal brand.

Lastly, you must also be clear about what kind of emotional temperament you show as an individual. You can be laidback, intense, fierce or cool as ice. Although this is an inherent attribute and it rarely changes unless someone is bent on changing it, you can try to reform it in a way that matches your personal brand.

WHAT KIND OF IMPACT DO YOU WANT TO MAKE?

B rands often focus on delivering a 'brand promise.' For most companies, a brand promise is the commitment to delivering value in a manner that is consistent with the expectation of its consumers. Companies also present this attribute as a brand purpose or brand mission.

Regardless, this purpose serves as an extension of the product's entire positioning. It is the attribute that brands want to be known for. As a result, it acts as the main agent for instilling brand loyalists with passion. For instance, Coca-Cola presents "inspiring moments of optimism and happiness" as a key part of its brand promise.

The same idea of a brand promise can help you a lot when you are defining your personal brand. If you are clear of what you want your associates to expect from you, it will be easier for you to influence the people around you.

However, for that, you need to look beyond selfish motives and realize what your mission should be in the role assigned to you. This can help you build positive memories with your colleagues and let them remember you long after you've moved onto another role. The impact you have on others serves as your legacy. Ultimately, having a strong personal brand will help you make a lasting impact on people who work with you.

Being a social network, LinkedIn provides you with the perfect opportunity to connect with people in your professional circle. However, when you are trying to build a strong personal brand, there's no harm in reaching out to people whom you don't have a direct correspondence with.

Many people wonder whether or not they should accept an invitation from a connection they don't really know. While many people avoid connecting with strangers on a platform like LinkedIn, that might be an opportunity to grow your influence as a professional.

It's no secret that having a powerful network can have a huge impact on how strong your personal brand will be. Engaging with your connections on LinkedIn can help boost your influence. Therefore, you need to focus on strengthening your network. Let's see how building a powerful network on LinkedIn can help improve your personal brand.

GROW YOUR NETWORK WISELY

To start off, you need to connect with people you know or trust. Therefore, you can connect with people that are outside your field of work. These people will be helpful in building the foundation of a strong network.

Furthermore, if your network has connections that you know personally, you can rely on these people to help you professionally. Regardless of whether you need an introduction, a job recommendation, or useful career advice, most of these people will be there for you.

While selecting people for your network, don't forget the people you have interacted with a lot. For instance, you should always add people you know from school, your previous workplace(s), or your college.

After that is done, you can connect with the people who belong to your field of work or share professional interests with. These people may have similar struggles as you have, which is why they can relate to your problems. Therefore, it is relatively easier to connect with them on a personal level.

Adding these people will help you stay informed about the latest opportunities in your industry.

When this is done, you can start seeking professionals that have mutual connections with people you are already connected with. Connecting with these people and engaging them through online activity can help you open new doors and avail opportunities, which you couldn't have in normal circumstances.

CHOOSE QUALITY OVER QUANTITY

Many people think that adding countless people to their LinkedIn account can boost their network and, thus, help them gain greater influence among their peers. However, that is not always the case. The number of connections isn't as important when compared to the kind of people you have added to your network.

You may have hundreds of connections on your LinkedIn profile. But, it's possible that none of them gives you the assistance you need. Therefore, the main goal of building your network on LinkedIn is to connect with people who understand your goals. It's important to add connections that can add value to your network or vice versa.

NURTURE YOUR NETWORK

While building your network, you should keep in mind that connections can go both ways. It's essential to connect with people you aspire to become, but being helpful to people who are not as experienced as you are can also be an enriching experience.

You have the option to make yourself available to others by maintaining regular conversations with your peers, mentors, or subordinates. LinkedIn provides you with several ways to do that. One of the most useful features in this aspect is Career Advice.

The Career Advice feature helps professionals to reach out to people who can give them valuable feedback from professionals that have plenty of knowledge to share. Similarly, if you have relevant knowledge and mastery of a subject, you can use Career Advice as a way to engage with people who can benefit from your knowledge. As a result, you will be able to gain devoted followers from your network.

Leveraging LinkedIn Groups

It's not easy to build a personal brand from scratch. Therefore, you need all the help you can get to utilize every option available on the platform. Some of the most useful features in this respect are LinkedIn Groups and company pages. You can use both of these platforms to engage with people who you want to learn from or interact with.

LinkedIn has millions of groups, each of which caters to users belonging to a certain category of professionals. These groups serve as a great platform, sharing content and ideas. Furthermore, they also act as another way to identify and form meaningful connections with the people you don't know.

To join groups where you can meet people with shared interests, you can make use of targeted keywords that relate to your interests and your goals. For instance, if you are seeking to connect with the people related to finance, you could directly search for groups related to your desired role. Enter keywords such as 'Finance', 'Accounting', 'CFO', 'Banking Careers', etc., to find a group you can benefit from. The search results from these keywords will give you useful insights into the group's structure and also tell you how large it is.

LinkedIn allows you to join as many as 50 groups if you are using a free account. However, some of these groups have a restriction on who can join them. Therefore, you would need the approval of the moderators of the groups in order to join them.

However, you should remember that not every group will live up to your expectations. Still, you need to join a group to find out whether a particular group is worth your time and effort. Over time, you will be able to find a group that aligns with your interests. Once you do that, you can use the group to propel your personal brand even more.

Nevertheless, the question remains: how can you take advantage of these groups to polish your personal brand? Let us see how LinkedIn groups can be helpful.

CONNECT WITH YOUR PEERS

Needless to say, people who join groups on LinkedIn want to interact with the people they share their interests with. Therefore, they are more interested in interacting with people on the same forum. This makes LinkedIn the perfect forum to connect with people with whom you share the same professional interests and goals.

Interacting with these people can help you to understand what kind of people work in your industry. By observing their behavior in these groups, you can have a fair idea of what you need to improve on. Furthermore, you can also observe the attributes that most of your peers lack and how gaining these traits can help you stand out.

KNOWLEDGE SHARING

Some of the most common things you'll see in LinkedIn groups are discussion posts related to certain aspects of your industry. By joining these groups, you can keep yourself updated with the latest trends in your field.

With so much competition in your professional field, it's important for you to keep your hand on the pulse of your industry. Missing out on key events and technological advancements can make your role irrelevant if you're not careful.

These groups are a reliable way to stay up-to-date with all the recent developments. You can use the knowledge gained from these groups to improve as a professional and prepare yourself for the coming changes.

ESTABLISH YOURSELF AS A THOUGHT LEADER

The usefulness of LinkedIn groups is just not limited to observing other people and improving your skills. You can also utilize these groups to launch yourself as a thought leader among your followers or community. These groups give you the perfect platform for doing that.

To become a useful resource or a thought leader in your group, you need to contribute to group discussions as much as you can. People who comment on group discussions can get as much as four times more profile views. The increasing number of views on your profile can lead to greater visibility of your personal brand.

The great thing about this approach is that it isn't that difficult to implement. Doing simple things such as answering questions asked by others or directing people to useful resources can go a long way in improving your standing in the group.

The point to take home here is to share valuable information with the people on these shares as it can help you get more attention than comments made just for the sake of attention. As long as you are useful to other people, your effort in the group will help you emerge as a thought leader. Consequently, it will also increase your influence as a professional.

ENGAGE WITH COMPANIES

T hink about the groups you want to give your time and attention to. However, once you find the right group, you will be able to get more opportunities for advancement in your field of interest.

Many employers keep their eyes on these groups to find the candidates they are looking for. These groups allow companies to observe the behavior of group members closely. Therefore, if you are participating in insightful conversations or sharing knowledge with other people on these groups, you can easily get the attention of these companies and stand out as a worthy candidate for a respective role.

However, if you want to join a LinkedIn group with the sole purpose of engaging with various companies, following a company page will be far more useful for this purpose. Here too, your interaction with other members of the company page will reflect your knowledge on the industry.

Crafting Content That Will Get You Noticed

We mentioned earlier how sharing authentic and useful knowledge with others is an effective way to stand out from the crowd. However, commenting on discussion posts or interacting with the company page offers limited opportunities to showcase your knowledge. If you really want people to know your insights on the key aspects of your industry, creating content related to those subjects will be far more effective.

LinkedIn gives you the opportunity to share specialized information directly with the people who are seeking it. One of the best tools that LinkedIn provides for personal branding is articles, which you can post on your profile, page, or group.

Moreover, you have the freedom to write about anything you're genuinely interested in. Your content piece can be about your personal experiences, your professional opinion, or your knowledge of a particular subject, as long as it gives value to other people.

Many people don't realize how writing LinkedIn articles can help them build and propagate their personal brands successfully. These articles not only represent the level of knowledge you have in a certain subject, but also give people a peek inside your mind. People associate your words, your style of writing, and your method of delivery with your personality.

Let us see how writing articles can help you bolster your personal brand.

KNOWLEDGE REPRESENTATION

A LinkedIn article is not a Facebook post update. When crafting a LinkedIn article, remember that you are writing for professionals. Therefore, whatever you write about, it should be based on facts and portray your area of expertise. However, expert writers use this opportunity to reveal their unique take on the subject.

This can help them represent a different outlook on common things. For instance, when a corporate professional creates content on 'the best practices before an interview', he or she can provide an example from their personal experience to offer useful insight to the readers.

Whatever you choose to write will show how deeply you assess situations. Furthermore, it will represent the extent of your knowledge on a subject matter and how informed you are about the latest trends in your respective field.

Having said that, it's important to remember that your article shouldn't be so specialized that your peers struggle to understand it. Make sure your content is easy-to-read, relevant, and to the point. If you don't follow these rules, you might not get the attention of your target audience.

BOOST YOUR ENGAGEMENT LEVEL

Writing content is the perfect way to stay in the spotlight on LinkedIn. Whenever members publish an article on a subject matter, LinkedIn informs their connections about it via notifications. This makes articles the perfect tool to spread the word about your personal brand among your connections in order to increase your influence.

INFLUENCE PEOPLE OUTSIDE YOUR NETWORK

The great thing about writing your own content on LinkedIn is that it's a closely-knit platform of professionals. Therefore, publishing articles on LinkedIn allows you to reach out to professionals, even without directly connecting with them.

LinkedIn articles are extremely easy to share. Members only need to search the right keywords in order to find hundreds of relevant articles on the subject they want to learn about. This can be advantageous for a person who wants to propel his or her personal brand on LinkedIn because when people share your article, they also share your personal brand.

However, to ensure your articles are worth sharing, you need to write informative articles that offer value to the readers. People won't share your articles unless they gain something from it. Furthermore, you need to invest your time in finding the right keywords for your content. Using searchable keywords in your content makes it more likely to be seen by people outside your network.

After creating informative content, work on making it more engaging for your audience. By making your content more engaging, you can persuade people to like, comment, and share your article, garnering more attention in the process. As a result, you can start influencing people outside of your network.

MAINTAIN A STRONG ONLINE PRESENCE

P osting articles on LinkedIn can assist you in maintaining a strong online presence. It's far too common to view a person's profile on LinkedIn and find no recent updates on it. As a result, people have the perception that your profile is usually inactive on LinkedIn.

In contrast, if your connections regularly see your content on their newsfeeds and see that you are active, they are more likely to interact with you. The same principle applies to people who only get to see you through your profile or the content you write. By constantly writing quality content, you can show that you are an active member who is ready to engage with the people offering the opportunities.

BECOME A BETTER WRITER

I deally, you should write about things you know about. Even if your first few articles don't make the impact you want them to make, you can use it as an opportunity to identify the mistakes you made.

Taking care of simple things can drastically improve your writing and help you connect with your targeted audience. For instance, if you are able to include an eye-catching feature image or write an engaging title for the article, you can positively influence the response rate.

It's important to be creative and keep the current topics in mind when writing for LinkedIn. With time, your writing will improve, and you will get to interact with more people and become more known.

Gathering Skill Endorsements and Recommendations

Some time ago, LinkedIn introduced skill endorsements and recommendations. Both these features allow members to verify their professional skills and endorse other members' skills. You can use both of these features to project a powerful personal brand image.

WHY ENDORSEMENTS MATTER

I f you want to build an authentic personal brand for yourself, getting endorsements from your manager (current or former), colleague, etc., is one way to do so. However, you need to limit these endorsements to a certain level. If your LinkedIn profile has unlimited skill endorsements from random people, it may give the impression that these endorsements are fake.

Therefore, you should keep an eye on the endorsements shown on your profile. Choose the endorsements carefully; make sure they reflect your true skills.

Moreover, there are other reasons for limiting the visibility of endorsements. One of these reasons is that the faces of your 12 most recent endorsers will be displayed on your profile. If you want your skills to seen as authentic, it's important to pick the most influential people to represent those skills.

Similarly, you can choose to include or exclude skill endorsements, based on the kind of brand you are representing. For instance, if you are into mobile application development, getting an endorsement from an experienced colleague or your manager can help validate your skills.

You can add 50 skills to your profile on a free account, so you can add as many skills as you want and you may even get endorsements for all of them. However, you might receive skill endorsements that don't represent your brand. In such a case, you can delete the skills that don't align with your brand values.

While LinkedIn endorsements work well for self-promotion, they can also act as an excellent tool for receiving invaluable feedback from your network. To get the most out of this feature, make sure to select endorsements that best represent your capabilities.

WHY ARE RECOMMENDATIONS BETTER?

S o far, we know that endorsements are a great way to validate your skills as long as you manage them carefully. However, you can endorse an individual's skills with the click of a button and require little effort. This is why many recruiters give preference to LinkedIn recommendations instead of endorsements.

Recommendations on LinkedIn are statements written by 1st-degree connections in your network. These recommendations are written to commend the individual they are being written for. Needless to say, recommendations are the perfect way of endorsing your personal brand on LinkedIn.

Whenever someone visits your profile, he or she will always read the recommendations you have received from your connections. They serve as a way of validating your personal values and your skills.

Anyone who has worked with you can write a recommendation for you. However, it's best that they are written by people who personally know you and understand the key aspects of your personal brand.

To receive a recommendation, you need to request your connections to write one for you. If your connection responds to your request and writes a recommendation for you, LinkedIn will notify you via a message from the person who wrote the recommendation.

Once you accept the recommendation, it will be displayed on your profile. You must remember that hiring managers and business partners prefer recommendations from the people they know and trust. Therefore, you must ensure that your recommendations are not only genuine but are also from distinguished people in your network.

After you accept the recommendation, it will appear on your profile by default. However, just like LinkedIn endorsements, you have the option to choose the recommendations you want to add to your profile. If you not satisfied with a recommendation, you can hide it or request your connection to change it up a bit.

Nevertheless, you need to be careful about who you ask to write a recommendation for you. Often, recruiters come across recommendations and may directly ask you about the person who had recommended you on LinkedIn.

Another thing you should keep in mind is to avoid recommendations that are vague or do not sound professional. For instance, if your recommendation says something like, *"It's a pleasure to work with John, he gets along with people, and I recommend him"*, then it is best to not add it to your profile as it does not add value to your brand and won't make much of an impact on potential recruiters.

To receive a recommendation that elevates your personal brand, you must request your connection to include keywords related to your brand. To solidify the authenticity of your brand, your connections can elaborate on when you displayed those traits while working with them.

They can highlight certain aspects of your professional capabilities, such as your ability to negotiate, your unrelenting work ethic, or your natural ability to resolve conflicts. However, be thankful to those who write recommendations for you and do the same for them if you could.